Rabboni

The School of His Rest
2016

Jesus is *Rabboni* our Teacher

Rabboni

The School of His Rest

2016

All Scriptures taken from the King James Bible and the Amplified Bible

Blessings to all who supported the completion of this assignment
Estelle Taylor and W.C.T.T.P., Joyce Taylor, Joyce Shipley, Bob and
Ann McMahon, Barney L. Christie, Anthony Christie, Margaret Brown
and the Prayer Clinic Team, and The Master's Table Family

Rabboni: The School of *His* Rest Volume no.1 555 Media Publishing
©2015 All Rights Reserved
Reproduction/Duplication without expressed consent from
Richard Taylor/555 media strictly prohibited by applicable Laws

THIS IS THE HOUR

TO

LIVE IN HIS GLORY

REST

Table of Contents

Why the School of His Rest?	5
Regulated by Glory	11
The Fear Factor	15
Just Come	22
Kryptonite	25
His Rest is Glorious	33
Like an Ocean Deep	39
Proclamations	43
Welcome Page	45
Class #1 Encounter	47
Class #2 Mindlessness	56
Class #3 Weightlessness	60
Class #4 Timelessness	71
Class #5 Procrastination	77
Class #6 Perfectionism	79
Class #7 Fearlessness	86
Healing Rest	91

**Please pause your reading during waiting times, this is first a School of Encounter. We want to see you arriving at Jesus feet receiving His Glorious Rest.
Thank you Lord!**

WHY THE SCHOOL OF HIS REST?

Thus said the LORD, The heaven is my throne, and the earth is my footstool: where is the house that you build to me? and **where is the place of my rest?** Isaiah 66:1

Here, we see God Himself enthroned in Rest, seated in Heaven; His feet reclining upon the earth (His footstool)… Yet He asks the question, where is the house that you build to me, and *where is the place of my Rest?* Solomon's answer was to build Him a Temple, but there was a further desire within the heart of God. This passage spoke to me deeply about God's desire for a *"Place of His Rest"*, and for His People to have a *"Place of His Rest"*. Ultimately that place is within us, as we are called to be the habitation of His Rest. The Rabboni School of His Rest is not an attempt to erect another earthly house as a container for His Rest, it is a School of Encounter whereby we may all become the Habitation of His Rest.

While some of our Churches can be great sources of strength and temporary relief from life's burdens, *His Rest* is rarely encountered within them (in fullness), experienced tangibly (in glorious manifestation), or fully understood (it cannot be fully understood without *encounter*).

For centuries the majority of the Church has underestimated the power of **His Rest**. It has been treated rather abstractly, or as a secondary spiritual supplement. For lack of transcendent testimony or encounter with **His Rest**, it has rarely been highlighted in our preaching and teaching. Subsequently, it has remained an undiscovered treasure. **His Rest** is perhaps the most powerful and vital end-time substance and adorning available to the Church! For me, it is a *Rock of Revelation,* a foundational truth that supports and undergirds many other spiritual truths. If this is so, why have we so grossly overlooked this incredible and Glory-filled substance?

Rest just sounds too ordinary!

Jesus was and is extraordinary. Everything he did was extraordinary (His miracles, healings, teachings, etc.). The way he loved unparalleled. *His birth was* unprecedented, *His life*, *His death*, *His Resurrection*, *Ascension*, *Intercession*, *and Righteousness are all* unprecedented, unparalleled, and extraordinary! How could *His Rest* be any different? Yet for the majority of my 26 years as a believer in Jesus Christ, I have witnessed and personally experienced the ravaging effects of unrest, fear and disorder, both in my own life, and in the lives of countless others.

I concluded that there could only be two possible reasons for this unfortunate phenomenon. Either His Rest was not to be taken literally, that it was more concept than reality, or that there was something missing in my own experience; something I needed to "learn of him".

While walking through several personal tribulations in recent years, suffering unimaginable fears and snares within, I had an amazing encounter with His Rest (See my testimonies). [*This was a monumental discovery that has had a massive impact on my life*] Jesus Christ revealed to me, and manifested within me, the power, potential and magnitude of *His Rest*. These were the beginnings of what I "learned of Him".

1. *His Rest flows out from His being, much like His Love.*
2. *It is of a much higher quality and order than it's human counterpart. (There's nothing comparable to it in the earth)*
3. *It can only minimally be attained through knowledge; knowledge simply increases our faith and opens the door to encounter. Pay special attention to the overview pages between the chapters in the School of Rest.*
4. *It can be transferred in a measure through impartation, often with amazing results*
5. *The Ultimate place of His Rest is within us*

In order for us to begin to understand it's amazing power and potential, we must first observe the words of the Prophet Isaiah:

And in that day there shall be a root of Jesse, which shall stand for an ensign of the people; to it shall the Gentiles seek: and his rest shall be *glorious. **Isaiah 11:10**

*The Hebrew word translated as *glorious* is *Kabod*, meaning *Glory*. Glory is God's weighty presence! The word glorious is substituted here to help the vernacular, but by doing so it vastly reduces our understanding of it's power. Let's look at this same scripture in the amplified bible.

*And it shall be in that day that the Root of Jesse (Jesus) shall stand as a signal for the peoples; of Him shall the nations inquire and seek knowledge, and **<u>His dwelling</u>** shall be **<u>glory</u>** (**His rest glorious**)*   **Isaiah 11:10 Amp. Bible (C)**

All who came to Jesus Christ with right motives received a manifestation of His Rest
These are all manifestations of unrest

- **When he encountered the demon possessed**
- **When he encountered the sick**
- **When he encountered the condemned**
- **When he encountered the fearful**
- **When he encountered the broken**
- **When he encountered the Hungry**
- **When he cleansed the Lepers**
- **All Life changing**
- **All miraculous**

This is your time of encounter
The School of His Rest is a School of Encounter
with an Illuminated Curriculum

Their Redeemer *is* strong; the LORD of hosts *is* his name: he shall throughly plead their cause, that he **<u>may give rest to the land...</u>**

Jeremiah 50:34

Jesus has been interceding for you, he is giving Rest to your land today!

IT'S WAITING TIME

SAY THIS WITH ME
"LORD I'M COMING FOR YOUR REST"

PLEASE DON'T FEEL GUILTY
HE GAVE YOU THE INVITATION

"COME UNTO ME ALL YE THAT LABOR, AND ARE
HEAVY LAIDEN, AND I WILL GIVE YOU REST"
MATTHEW 11:28

PREPARE FOR YOUR ENCOUNTER

Lord I pray for a Supernatural Encounter with you in your Rest as your people wait in your presence. Touch Lord with your tangible Glory and move upon each life. I release to you by Apostolic Grace the Gift of Faith to receive the Substance of His Rest in tangible manifestation as your initial measure...

Reach now for Jesus Christ our Savior for the fullness of His Rest, and continue to enlarge and infill the Bubble

(Extend your Spirit to Him)

What is the Bubble?

The Bubble is a perimeter that the Rest of God establishes around your life that is very tangible. The Rest first manifests within, but then there often comes a very real sense of protection from all forms of unrest that forms around us. When His Rest is encountered, many have experienced this phenomenon. Rest within and without. One woman described it as a bubble, so we liked it and named it so. It is simply a manifestation of The Rest of the Lord Jesus Christ which effects the atmosphere directly around us,
His Rest is Glorious...

REGULATED BY GLORY

In Him we Live and Move

When given opportunity and invitation, God's Glory regulates life, atmosphere and light. Moses descended from Mt. Sinai in it, Jesus was transfigured before his disciples in it, and was again envisioned by John in it.

And in the midst of the seven candlesticks one like unto the Son of man, clothed with a garment down to the foot, and girt about the paps with a golden girdle. His head and his hairs were white like wool, as white as snow; and his eyes were as a flame of fire; And his feet like unto fine brass, as if they burned in a furnace; and his voice as the sound of many waters.

Revelation 1:13-15

This is clearly a picture of Jesus Glorified, but what are the candlesticks spoken of here?

The mystery of the seven stars which thou sawest in my right hand, and the seven golden candlesticks. The seven stars are the angels of the seven churches: and **the seven candlesticks which thou sawest are the seven churches.** **Revelation 1:20**

The prophetic picture that I see here is that Jesus will be Glorified in the midst of a people who are bringing forth light in the midst of darkness. That's what Candles do.

The Lord is coming to be Glorified in His Saints

*When he shall come to be glorified in his saints, and to be admired in all them that believe **(because our testimony among you was believed)** in that day.* **2 Thessalonians 1:10-12**

This speaks of a people who are shining with the Brightness of His Glory. He will come to be Glorified within them corporately and individually as they burn for him. They have believed the Apostolic and Prophetic testimony in their day, that which was intended to move them into a place of preparation and safety, positioning them as overcomers in the midst of world-wide suffering. <u>Have you yet believed, are you ready to be positioned?</u>

*And to you who are troubled **rest with us**, when the Lord Jesus shall be revealed from heaven with his mighty angels,*
2 Thessalonians 1:7

The end-time Apostolic and Prophetic ministry is charged with the mandate of calling, inviting and moving the people of God into His Rest, which they, themselves, have obtained.
Have you heard the call?

Now, like no other time in history, we, the people of God

must position ourselves in His Rest. Our programs, agendas, and human strategies for Church growth will prove but one thing. That we have the *Martha* syndrome, not having chosen that which was good (for the present hour we live in). If we will move out of the way, and allow the King of Glory to invade our meetings, lifestyles and daily routines, He will come to be Glorified and admired in our midst. He will regulate our lives by His Glory and Rest. Saints, this is the most important area of preparation for the end-times.

WE MUST ALL ENROLL IN THE SCHOOL OF HIS REST.

THE WATERS ARE RISING...

MEN'S HEARTS FAILING THEM FOR FEAR, AND FOR LOOKING AFTER THOSE THINGS WHICH ARE COMING UPON THE EARTH: FOR THE POWERS OF HEAVEN SHALL BE SHAKEN

LUKE 21:26

THE FEAR FACTOR

(CONDITIONED TO RESPOND AND NOT REACT)

During a recent ministry trip to Oregon in late 2015, on one rainy evening, I witnessed two hawks flying through the rain and winds majestically. These birds were not flapping haplessly through the storm, reacting to the undesirable weather, they were responding to it with great Grace and Strength. This was a first for me, as I had never seen a hawk flying through a storm. They were likely caught off guard by the inclement weather, and had no opportunity to rise above the clouds. This said to me that Storms will arise quickly in these times, and that we must be prepared beforehand.

Immediately after seeing this, I heard the words "Fair Weather Eagles". The clear message to me was that we can all be Eagles on sunny days, when skies are blue, and there are no storms of life; but the Glory of those two hawks was manifested in the storm, as they cut through the elements in Rest.

Without the Glory and Rest of God, every believer will be exposed as a Fair Weather Eagle, haplessly unprepared for the coming atmospheric shifts. The world is experiencing the beginning of sorrows, the spiritual climate is not at all friendly, and the warfare is becoming increasingly more intense and unfamiliar. The winds of warfare have shifted. Principalities, like dark clouds, have been strategically relocated throughout the earth.

Our first responses to these end-time patterns of darkness

will set the course for all that is to follow. It's only natural to fear in times such as this. This is why the Lord is calling his people into an encounter with His Super-Natural Rest. When empowered by the Glory of His Rest, our strength will be ever-renewable, our spiritual resources (faith, hope, peace etc.) will be free to access without the crippling effects of fear, and our responses will be *borne* (to be carried or transported) of the Holy Spirit!

Mark 4:35-41

And there arose a great storm of wind, and the waves beat into the ship, so that it was now full. And he (Rabboni) was in the hinder part of the ship, asleep on a pillow:

Who could Rest on a ship filled with water? Who sleeps in the midst of a tempestuous storm? **Rabboni** does! And His Rest was the foundation for his controlled response. It (His Rest) was in control of the immediate atmosphere within and around him [His inner life saturated by Glory and Rest]. The care free zone, The Rest zone. It was from this place that he commanded peace.

and they awake him, and say unto him, **Master, carest thou not that we perish?**

These words were undoubtedly infused with fear, looking for something to grip. Have you ever been awakened by fear? The disciples, here, are gripped with fear and terror. As they awakened the Lord, we might have expected him to be traumatized by this assault on *His Rest*. But not so!

And he arose, and rebuked the wind, and said unto the sea, **Peace, be still.** *And the wind ceased, and there was a great calm.*

In a very real way Jesus "imparted" peace to the sea. And believe you me, if he could impart it into the vastness of the sea, he can impart it unto you. The vastness of the sea became subject unto the power of His Rest. You will notice that the command to "be still" was secondary, his first response to the sea was "Peace", from a position of Rest.

From the position of Rest, Rabboni was empowered to:

1. Rebuke the winds (and all of their vastness)
2. Impart Peace (into the Great Sea)
3. Still the sea (the vastness of the waters)

In a time such as this, when gifts have been so much of the emphasis in the Body of Christ, we really need to take another look at *Rabonni's* Life. Gifts are not the means by which we will stand. The disciples had already worked miracles at this point in their ministry training. Here on the ship, <u>they were enrolled in the School of His Rest!</u> Exposed as Fair Weather Eagles, unable to use their faith because of the absence of Rest! Everybody wants to be like Mike, I want to be Just like *Rabonni. Cool under pressure!*

Gifts are not for foundation, they are for use and function.

None of our spiritual weapons work very well when being released from a position of chaos and unrest. *Rabboni* is releasing a dynamic measure of His Supernatural Rest to all who will come unto him. An unshakeable foundation results in an unshakeable building!

We are the Lord's building!   **1 Corinthians 3:9**
Made from lively stones!   **1 Peter 2:5**

And he said unto them, Why are ye so fearful? how is it that ye have no faith? And they feared exceedingly, and said one to another, What manner of man is this, that even the wind and the sea obey him?

So few today understand the magnitude of His Rest; it is an end-time life preserver, and a Weapon of Divine Positioning over Fear and Death! When we are seated in Rest, we are seated in power! I dare to say that there is no singular need or substance more necessary and fundamental to our survival as Christians than His Rest (GLORY)... Without it, many will **Fold in the Fire.**

There will be an enormous *Fear Factor* during these end-times, which will determine the outcome of many things. His Rest is the substance that will clothe the *overcomers*. This is the substance that will sustain the oppressed, and empower the Church to stand and advance in this hour. This is the Glory that arrests all fear, yes, His Rest will be the hottest commodity of the end-times, as fear breeds and feeds on the multitudes.

Our Great Shepherd is releasing this Glory-filled substance of his being to all who will come; for he has seen the affliction of his people. He again weeps over a modern day Lazarus Company of suffering loved ones and friends. He has heard the groaning of the intercessors, and has seen the burden of the oppressed (believers and non-believers alike) ...Although the heavenly solution has long since been provided for, multitudes of people have yet to possess it. The Father loves every one of us so much, and He doesn't want us living our lives in bondage to fear [Hebrews 2:15].

Lord Jesus, we have heard your heart's cry! And now oh Lord, at long last, we are coming to *possess* your REST!

Come unto me all ye that labor and are heavy laiden,
and I will give you Rest...
Matthew 11:28

The LORD thy God in the midst of thee is mighty; he will save, he will rejoice over thee with joy; he will **rest** in his love, **he will joy over thee with singing.**

Zephaniah 3:17

Jesus has been interceding for you, he is giving Rest to your land today!

IT'S WAITING TIME AGAIN

SAY THIS WITH ME
"LORD I'M COMING FOR YOUR REST"

HE GAVE YOU THE INVITATION

"COME UNTO ME ALL YE THAT LABOR, AND ARE HEAVY LAIDEN, AND I WILL GIVE YOU REST, TAKE MY YOKE UPON YOU AND LEARN OF ME, FOR I AM MEEK AND LOWLY IN HEART, AND YOU SHALL FIND REST FOR YOUR SOULS"

MATTHEW 11:28-29

PREPARE FOR YOUR ENCOUNTER

Lord I pray for a Supernatural Encounter with you in your Rest as your people wait in your presence. Touch Lord with your tangible Glory and move upon each life. I release to you by Apostolic Grace the Gift of Faith to receive the Substance of His Rest in tangible manifestation as your initial measure...

Reach now for Jesus Christ our Savior for the fullness of His Rest, and continue to enlarge and infill the Bubble

(Extend your Spirit to Him)

JUST COME

In this, the second volume of His Rest, the initial focus will be on the act or process of Coming. This invitation to COME, is in and of itself a challenge for some of us. It is a directive, and we humans are not always good with God-Given directives. They are sometimes construed as religious, or routine, if not mundane or inconvenient. I can assure you that they are neither of these. God's directives are Life-Giving and Rescuing! This invitation is not being pushed on you, it's an offering of amazing compassion from the one who is touched with the feelings of your infirmities.
Amazing goodness awaits you.

The Lord wants us to let our guards down so that he can give us what he is drawing us for, and what we so desperately need. "Come unto me" is an invitation to all mankind to enter into the Rest Zone (The Reality of a life lived under the Dominion of the Rest/Glory of God). Yes, His Rest is our remedy.

The next directive is to TAKE His Yoke! Christ is literally saying that we need to stick our necks out in faith, and allow him to put them into the Yoke of His Rest! Relax, it's okay, the moment this yoke is attached to you, the freedom you have so desperately longed for begins! And by the way, in case I didn't mention it, *FEAR* disappears when His Rest is received! When taking your very first steps, you may experience the presence of fear, this is quite normal. Just remember that Jesus is right there with you.

If you've never been yoked to His Rest, get excited, you are about to be personally discipled by *Rabboni* himself. He said, "*take my yoke upon you and **learn of me***", this is truly the opportunity of a lifetime. You will learn more about the Kingdom of God than you could have ever imagined because of the Dominion of His Rest. His Rest/Glory manifests an internal and external environment where every Kingdom Truth, Anointing, Promise, and Blessing is maximized for our benefit! You will actualize many things that you have only dreamed of before, and experience many things that have been held up, delayed or deferred.

When we are yoked to His Rest, we are yoked to Him, we are yoked to the Life of God's presence, and we experience a joining of Hearts.

"But he that is joined unto the Lord is one spirit"

1 Corinthians 6:17

Do you want to be yoked to Jesus? I do, every day of my life! When I am yoked to him, he removes the burdens of past and present failures, relationships, mistakes and hardships. These are burdens that are common to all of us. Jesus Christ, the Lamb of God, is the **Promise** of Rest (Isaiah 11:10), and the **Provision** for Rest (Matthew 11:28). So now, more than ever, it is time for us to retake **Possession** of the Glorious Rest of God in the person of Jesus Christ! !We have been given the greatest opportunity known to man, second only to Salvation/Eternal Life...*The recovery of His Rest! Just Come and be joined in one spirit, you can rest now...*

And my people shall dwell in a peaceable habitation, and in sure dwellings, and in quiet **resting places**;

Isaiah 32:18

Jesus has been interceding for you, he is giving Rest to your land today!

KRYPTONITE

The Rest Antagonist

Unrest is at such an all time high that many have turned to practicing Yoga, Hypnotism, and various forms of Eastern Meditation [which are spiritually ill-advised because of the openness they provide to demonic spirits], in order to escape the fury of anxiety and fear. These are lawless practices for God's people to partake of, and offer nothing in the same stratosphere as Christ's tangible Rest. Others have turned to vices, or prescription medications to ease the pain of unrest. [***Prescription medications should not be discontinued without consulting your physician, even when His Rest begins to manifest***]

Note: If you are practicing Yoga, Eastern meditation, New Age meditation, Reiki, Transcendental meditation, or any other forms of spirituality contrary to the Gospel of Jesus Christ, I encourage you to discontinue these practices now, before Reaching for His Rest. They are not approved by the Lord Jesus Christ, and may present a hindrance to you receiving His Rest! He wants you to receive His Rest more than you do! At the end of this segment, you will have an opportunity to renounce such practices and to break the power of every potential hindrance.

Testimony of Hindered Miracles and Rest

Several years ago I prayed for a woman who visited our

then home fellowship, and began to attend regularly. The more she came, the more we loved her. She had been referred to us because of her cancer diagnoses, and the visible golf ball sized tumor on her neck... The doctors had given her little or no chance to live.

When she first arrived at our door, she was very weak and frail, but miraculously, after only 2 weeks her golf ball sized tumor shrunk 98%. Yes it was as flat as a quarter, a clear miracle from God. In a very short time she grew stronger and showed more life and vigor. Not long after this, my wife and I visited her home with another couple from our Church. As we looked around, we discovered that her library was stocked full of books on Astrology, Tarot Cards, Buddhism, New Age, The Occult and other forms of demonic spiritual activity. As a matter of fact, we discovered that she had been going to a Licensed Buddhist Medical Practitioner and was paying $900.00 per hour to do so. Her home had become a demonic stronghold.

One of the ladies who went with us saw hundreds of serpents slithering on her floor in a vision. We immediately instructed her to throw away, (not give away), all of her books and visible crystals which were leftover inventory from a New Age Store once owned by herself and her husband..

Perhaps the most troubling event of our first visit happened while we sat at her dinner table. I began to experience unexplained sharp pains in my right arm; as this went on for a while, I heard the Lord speak to me and say "turn to your right". As I did this, I saw a huge crystal attached to what looked like the base of a trophy. On the crystal the word **KRYPTONITE** was inscribed on it's brass plate... Kryptonite was *the fictional mineral that made Superman Weak; it poisoned him.*

Well, there was a clear prophetic message being sent. She was surrounded by so many things that were draining the life out of her. But God is merciful, and revealed the sources.

A few weeks after my wife and I instructed her to discard all of her books, crystals, and the other New Age/Occult objects in her home, inexplicably, she began to take a turn for the worse in her health. We were both saddened and surprised at this regression. [We have seen God heal sick people of their diseases for over 25 years.]

We started to see her less and less at the meetings, and received a call from her daughter to come over to her house again. With all of our hearts we prayed for and loved on our dear sister. My wife played the harp and cried out to God for her life. Worship filled the air. As we were getting ready to leave, her daughter pulled us aside and said "I can't let this go on anymore, my mom is deceiving you". "She still goes to the Buddhist Practitioner, and she never threw any of those crystals away, they are in the basement in a box". "She said that they were too expensive to throw away, and that the *Kryptonite* crystal was worth over $1,000 dollars".

Though our sister told us that she threw everything away, she had actually rejected our counsel in favor of the Buddhist practitioner (and continued to see him), and kept all of her new age crystals (which were used to release various energies in hopes of healing her).

A short time later we were called in again as she was nearing her death. When we arrived at the hospital, and walked into her room, there stood a Witch chanting over her wearing a long black garment, and a two foot tall black hat with a wide brim. She was strewn with multi-colored bangles, and was introduced to us as one of her long time friends.(She literally looked like "The Wicked Witch of the West") The scene in the Hospital room could have been entitled "CONFUSION". Witches, Buddhist's, New Age Practitioners, Christians, Gnostics, etc., she had been looking for Rest in all the wrong places, but it could only be found in Jesus Christ!

Shortly thereafter, within the same hour, this dear sister made a life decision. She publicly renounced her previous New Age lifestyle of over 30 years, and asked that everyone except my wife, myself, and a brother named Peter be removed from her room. Before the room cleared, in front of her friends and family, she renounced the idols in her life, and confirmed her faith in Christ alone. This instigated a backlash from the Buddhist contingent in the room, but she was absolute in her resolve. The Spiritual Battle was won, and she entered into an amazing place of His Rest..

I was the only non-family member to see her in the last hours of her life. We spent time together rejoicing in the Lord, and in his wonderful and free gift of Eternal Life. I am convinced that she would have been completely healed had she removed the hindrances when she was instructed to. [These instructions were given by the Grace and Love of God, who wants only the best for His children]. Clearly the Lord had already began to Divinely heal her, having removed the large tumor from her neck. I believe that her disease was directly connected to the occult objects within her home. Her husband had died 3 years before her of the same disease, and they owned and managed a New Age business together. God is bigger than all of the idols, practices and potions offered as false sources of Rest. You wont need an object, a crystal or an idol...

Jesus makes it very clear...

"COME UNTO ME, ALL YE THAT LABOR AND ARE HEAVY LAIDEN, AND I WILL GIVE YOU REST"
Matthew 11:28

Prayer: Father God, I ask that you would free every person reading this book from every snare, bondage and stronghold of the enemy, that came in through participation in unlawful spiritual practices. I declare your freedom, and every hindrance broken in the name of the Lord Jesus Christ. Repeat this after me: I renounce the use of every unlawful spiritual practice (name them if you can). I resign my hope to, and place my faith in Jesus Christ, the source of God's True Rest.

Note: The Glory of His Rest is destructive to demonic forces when received in full measure, let me be clear, *nothing can stand in the presence of His Glory*! Now that you have renounced all known hindrances, and we have covered the remaining ones in prayer, you can expect to have an amazing encounter with His Rest. Tormenting spirits are traumatized by the Glory of His Rest, I am a living witness! There is a magnificent measure available to those who would seek the Lord for a further and deeper apprehending of His Rest. See my testimonies in the coming chapters, and reach for the Glory that arrests all fear.

PRAYER OF IMPARTATION

FATHER, I ask that you would endow every believer in Jesus Christ reading this book with the Gift of Faith. I pray that each one will be able to receive your Rest in full measure at the feet of Jesus Christ...Receive the Gift of Faith! I pray that every reader, Christian or not, has an amazing encounter with your Glorious Rest! Say goodbye to the Dominion of Fear once and for all, as His Rest manifests, you will know in yourself that you are free.

Move out of the realm of reason now, and into the Faith of God... Draw near, extend your spirit and receive His Rest

And the LORD gave them **rest** round about, according to all that he sware unto their fathers: and there stood not a man of all their enemies before them; the LORD delivered all their enemies **into their hand.**

Joshua 21:44

Jesus has been interceding for you, he is giving
Rest to your land today!

IT'S WAITING TIME AGAIN

SAY THIS WITH ME
"LORD I'M COMING FOR YOUR REST"

HE GAVE YOU THE INVITATION

YOU CAN REACH FOR HIS REST ANYTIME YOU DESIRE. HE'S AVAILABLE 24 HOURS A DAY. DON'T STOP REACHING UNTIL YOU FEEL THE WAVES OF HIS REST AND GLORY GOING OVER YOU, AND INTO YOU.

"COME UNTO ME ALL YE THAT LABOR, AND ARE HEAVY LAIDEN, AND I WILL GIVE YOU REST"
MATTHEW 11:28

BY NOW SURELY YOU BELIEVE, AS I DID, THAT HIS REST IS LITERAL AND MIRACULOUS, MORE TANGIBLE THAN FEAR COULD EVER BE...THIS IS THE REST OF JESUS CHRIST

PREPARE FOR YOUR ENCOUNTER...RECEIVE

Lord I pray for a Supernatural Encounter with you in your Rest as your people wait in your presence. Touch Lord with your tangible Glory and move upon each life. I release to you by Apostolic Grace the Gift of Faith to receive the Substance of His Rest in tangible manifestation as your initial measure...

Reach now for Jesus Christ our Savior for the fullness of His Rest, and continue to enlarge and infill the Bubble

(Extend your Spirit to Him)

HIS REST IS GLORIOUS

Testimony of My first encounter

It was an early afternoon while I was rereading some of my spiritual notes on Rest. That day I was inspired by God to apply what I was reading, to simply come to Jesus for His Rest! I clearly remember that my faith had risen to a level of great expectation, and I was eager to meet the Lord. I had been in a long term battle with fear, and was in the late rounds of the fight... Although I was standing my ground, I was not winning the battle. Blow after blow, fear struck me, taking it's toll (compete unrest) on my soul.

I am convinced that it was the Holy Spirit that directed me to read my own notes that day, and while I was reading, the *reality* that I could touch the Lord as easily as I could turn on a light switch arrived in my spirit. [You might say that I received the Gift of Faith prior to this encounter]. This Faith arrived as I read through some of the contents of this book. With renewed faith, I got up from my computer, and went and laid down on my side in quietness. Shortly after this, my cell phone rang, and I remember my spirit being extremely grieved at the interruption. [I had already begun to experience His Rest in a measure, but wasn't really aware of it] Who was calling me at a time like this?

Note: If you are serious about obtaining His Rest, you will have to take measures to remove all distractions, people, cell phones, music, etc., if at all possible.

As I laid there on my bed, I simply said "Lord, I am coming for your Rest". After waiting for maybe two or three minutes, there were no waves of rest that I could recognize, but my faith was fixed on him. "Lord, I'm coming for your Rest", I repeated, and again there was nothing to speak of in terms of a change in my state of rest or peace... Now at this point, many of us would have just given up, saying to ourselves "He didn't really mean that I should come unto him, and that he would *literally* give me rest", or "This may work for some people, but it won't work for me". Well, these statements are born from unbelief, and unbelief stops us from entering into the promise of Rest.

And to whom sware he that they should not enter into his rest, but to them that believed not? **Hebrews 3:18**

Note: Everything that I needed in order to believe was provided by the Lord himself. He gave me the notes, led me to read them, and filled me with faith to come unto him for Rest. Just like he did it for Peter, he will do it for you...Walk out on His Word and COME! This book will provide more than enough faith and focus to COME, it contains my notes. Make sure to follow my example as you continue to read…

That ye be not slothful, but followers of them who through faith and patience inherit (possess) the promises. **Hebrews 6:12**

Well, I must say that although nothing seemed to change, my faith was still at a very high level of expectation. With the support of this new found faith, I said it again, "Lord Jesus, I am coming for your Rest". As I said this, I reached for him as an act of faith with my total inner being, spirit and soul in one accord.

While reaching, [extending my spirit to him] ***I immediately arrived at the feet of Jesus Christ.*** He was not in my room, that I know of, it was as if I had been brought into the chambers of the King. All I needed to do was come. I didn't speak a word, nor do I remember him speaking. All that I can say about this encounter was that "His Rest Is Glorious"! I was infused from head to toe with a substance so wonderful, so overwhelming, so transforming, so neutralizing to everything that opposes it, that I did not want to move or lose the reality of it. I actually lost consciousness of everything that I needed spiritually, physically and emotionally. I had no prayer requests, no needs or troubles at all... Rest had dealt with all things, and brought order where there once was chaos.

I experienced enormous peace, but it was more than peace...it was as if I was living in a Garden called Eden, before the age of knowledge, naked and unashamed (all things were new).

After what was probably no more than a half an hour (though I really lost track of time), I remember getting up from my bed a free man. But more than free, I was filled and surrounded by the Rest of God. My perceptions of time and space were altered. My sensitivities where heightened and maximized. As I prepared to take my daily walk, everything seemed to slow down to a snails pace. While walking, it literally seemed as if the cars where travelling at 10-15 miles per hour, and that time was running at half-speed. I was moving under the Dominion of Rest, and the Dominion of Fear had been broken and removed.

I remained under the shadow of God's Glory and Rest for about two and a half months as result of this one encounter with His Rest. This encounter with the Rest of the Lord Jesus Christ transformed my life, and made quick work of Fear. I gained more freedom in a half hour than could have been accomplished through a hundred hours of study, or a thousand declarations of faith. For this, oh Lord, I am forever grateful. Your Rest is *Glory*!

The Lord revealed many things to me in the days just after this encounter. I would like to share them with you:

Warnings from the Lord after receiving His Rest

1.) *That I must continue to come unto to him to maintain this Rest (a key to remaining free from fear)*
2.) *That His Rest is available to <u>all</u> who come to him in faith*
3.) *That I could impart His Rest in a measure to others, and that it would manifest as an anointing upon me, and I presume for anyone that goes directly to the source, Jesus Christ*
4.) *That I am to always point people to him, in order to obtain this rest for themselves, but that I could give them an initial measure as a literal "boost" for their souls*
5.) *Not to allow anyone to become dependant upon the measure that was imparted to me, but to send them to the source which is he*

himself

6.) That he wanted all of his people (worldwide) to receive His Glorious Rest as a first line of defense against the numerous troubles and sorrows of these last days

7.) That some would underestimate the power of His Rest, and fail to come to him for this Glory-filled substance of his being. This would become a sorrow of his own Heart. He is releasing His Rest as perhaps the most vital divine substance, endowment and gratuity of the end-times.

Note: In coming for His Rest, let nothing discourage you…If during the first "coming" there is not an instant manifestation, come again! I had to come multiple times at first! His Rest is working whether you feel it or not. The Breakthrough will suddenly or eventually come from the depths of your spirit and soul. When His Rest arrives in fullness (and registers with your senses), you may be involved in another activity altogether… But when it comes, you will feel the waves!

If you would like to (COME) now for His Rest, proceed to the Chapter R.E.A.C.H.. Or read on and *come* when you're ready.

*Return unto thy **rest**, O my soul; for the LORD hath dealt* **<u>bountifully with thee.</u>**

Psalms 116:7

Jesus has been interceding for you, he is giving Rest to your land today!

LIKE AN OCEAN DEEP

"Learn of me"

After such an incredible initial experience with His Rest, I had great expectations for my next encounter. I soon found out that I was still enrolled in the School of His Rest, each and every day "learning of him". In my first encounter, I experienced the power of great waves of Rest flowing over me, very much like these verses in Psalm 42.

Deep calleth unto deep at the noise of thy waterspouts: all thy waves and thy billows are gone over me. **Psalms 42:7**

As the waves of God's Glory and Rest crash over us, we experience a phenomenon I call "adaptation". When His Glorious Rest rolled over my being, I adapted to it, and not the other way around. His Rest made me whole, adjusted my soul, and replenished my spirit. All I had to do was "yield", and I was changed! Yes changed, not encouraged, though I am encouraged. No, this was not a "pick me up", or a "flash flood" that quickly dried up. This was an Ocean, and I was the fish, surrounded and sustained by the life of the deep, deep, Rest of God.

My first encounter set the bar really high, and for some time I expected to experience His Rest in the same way or degree. It is most important that we continue to Come unto our Lord to obtain

His Glorious Rest. He wants us to walk in the full measure of it for all of our days here on earth.

After several "Comings", I was woefully aware that I was not experiencing the same level of impact or encounter with His Rest. This initially discouraged me, but I continued to pursue it/ Him. During my pursuit, the Holy Spirit revealed to me that I had been *forever changed* by my first encounter with His Rest. This truth would be **the key to opening the door for my next encounter**. I then understood why the impact seemed lesser, it wasn't His Rest that had changed, it was me! I had already adapted to the substance and lifestyle of Rest.

My next discoveries were amazing, and truly encouraging. There came an increase in "learning of him".

One late afternoon after working on one project or another, I distinctly remember a low level sensation of unrest trying to set in against me. Normally I would just press through it and brush it off, or simply say "Lord, I receive your Rest". But this time, I remember being moved to go and lay down to rest my body for a while. While laying down, I decided to use that time as an opportunity to Reach for His Rest. As I reached, it felt like I was inserting a key into a door, and when the first key didn't fit, I tried a second key. Amazingly, I walked right in, I felt the wave again! Much to my surprise, I was able to move into greater depths of His Rest at will; now this was a new experience for me, and once again, I was "learning of him". The Lord was teaching me how to "lay hold of" His Rest *before* I felt it's liberating effect on my soul. It was so easy after this, Jesus is such an amazing teacher!

Now faith is the assurance (the confirmation, [a] the title deed) of the things [we] hope for, being the proof of things [we] do not see and the conviction of their reality [faith perceiving as real fact what is <u>not revealed to the senses</u>]. **Hebrews 11:1 Amp**

Just like Peter walking on the water, my first encounter with His Rest was "new" and "overwhelming", "transforming" in so many ways. We don't know if Peter ever attempted to walk on water again, but I am sure that if hid did, he would have "learned of him" and perfected the process. The Lord is teaching me more and perfecting the process of obtaining His Rest. I am more confident to walk on the waters, my faith has been matured in the pursuit of His *Miraculous* Rest. Even when the waters of life are turbulent and raging, I have been enabled by the Lord to walk and not faint.

This assurance of faith makes His Rest accessible NOW! I really (now) believe that I am always connected to the Lord and His Rest, but I still set apart times of refreshing in the presence of the Lord. These times ensure that a full measure of His Glorious Rest saturates my soul and resonates within my being. Lord Jesus, I thank you for teaching me how to obtain and abide in your Glorious Rest!

Enroll in the School of His Rest today. The classes are free, and the Teacher is awesome. His name is Jesus Christ! Warning: counterfeits abound, there are many false Christ's (saviors, healers, peace givers, etc.) but don't believe them. There is only one source of the True Rest of God; It is our Lord Jesus Christ!

*I will gather them that are sorrowful for the solemn assembly, who are of thee, to whom the reproach of it was a burden. Behold, at that time I will undo all that afflict thee: and I will save her that halteth (limps), and gather her that was driven out; and I will get them praise and fame in every land where they have been put to shame...***when I turn back your captivity before your eyes, saith the LORD.**

Zephaniah 3:18-20

Jesus has been interceding for you, he is giving Rest to your land today!

PROCLAIMATIONS

Proclamation: The winds and the seas of tribulation must cease from functioning in my life by the authority of the Rest of Jesus Christ! I open my heart wide right now and receive Rabboni's Rest! The stillness of God is manifesting throughout my being in Rest; in the name of Jesus Christ! "I receive His Rest"... "I receive His Rest"... "I receive His Rest..." "I receive the Rest of the Lord Jesus Christ". Once again "I receive the Rest of the Lord Jesus Christ"! "I release all fear and anxiety by the power of His Rest"

Now Breathe...abide, abide in Him, abide in the calming Glory of His Rest...Glory of His Rest be released into every system, every cell, every atom, every realm of your being...

Declare this directly into your storm with me: "Peace be still, Peace be still, I command by the Rest of the Lord Jesus Christ, Peace be still. Emotions be still, Emotions be still, I command by the Rest of the Lord Jesus Christ, Emotions be still"

Meditation: The Glory of His Rest is the supernatural manifestation of God's weighty presence lifting me up and removing my every burden and weight...Christ *The Annointed One, Now Glorified, breaks every yoke of unrest* (We bless your life with Rest in the name of the Lord Jesus Christ the Messiah) He is the

Rosh vaSof (The beginning and the ending) Revelation 1:8... The *Lechem Shemayim* (The Bread of Heaven) John 6:32... abide in His Rest...

The winds and the seas always respond to the Word of His Rest. When combining these two words, Rest and Order we get the word *Restored, or Restored Order*! The Glory of God regulating every aspect of life, manifesting in Rest and Order. We command **Restored Order** to your mind, your soul, your spirit and your body, in the name of the Lord Jesus Christ..

Proclaim this with me: I receive restored order to my mind, my soul, my spirit and my body in the name of the Lord Jesus Christ..

In the coming chapters we will focus much more on impartation of the Glory and Rest of God which is much more to be manifested than it is to be expounded on

WELCOME TO
THE RABBONI SCHOOL OF HIS REST

Now that you have read through the preliminaries, you are ready to begin the classes.

It is our sincere desire that each enrollee becomes a man or woman of Rest; obtaining His Rest in full measure; releasing His Rest to the Nations...

THE MAN OF REST

Behold, a son shall be born to thee, who shall be a man of rest; and I will give him rest from all his enemies round about: for his name shall be Solomon, and I will give peace and quietness unto Israel in his days.

1 Chronicles 22:9

The RABBONI SCHOOL *of* His Rest

SCHOOL'S IN SESSION

Relax Extend Access Come Heal

Class #1 | Encounter

The Lord is inviting every soul to come unto him and to receive his rest. This is more than an invitation to forgiveness, it is a journey into the Glorious Liberty of the Children of God! Most literally, Jesus is bidding you to COME into an actual encounter with a profound aspect of his nature, and a remarkable substance of his being...*REST/GLORY.*

> *...who (Jesus) being the brightness of his (God's) glory*
> **Hebrews 1:3**

Relax; **(Go to a quiet place if possible)** he wants you to receive this rest more than you do. The doors of love are always open, 24 hours a day you can come. There's never an inconvenient time to come, never an inconvenient hour. **Remove every earthly/physical distraction** (cell phones, music, TV's, other people, etc.), and **commit** to press through the crowd of mental and emotional distractions (intrusive thoughts, imaginations, etc.). **Lie down or sit down** (be positioned for Rest), and see yourself approaching the Lord (through the eyes of your faith).

I now impart unto you an initial measure of His Rest to break the dominion of restlessness in the name of the Lord Jesus Christ. Say this with me, *"I receive the Rest of the Lord Jesus*

Christ"...Say it with me one more time, *"I receive the Rest of the Lord Jesus Christ"*...

The details of your encounter may differ from mine, he is without limitation, he is incomparable in power, transcendent in Glory, and eager to meet with you... Remember, the flesh is very impatient, but wait and reach. Faith and patience must partner together in this pursuit of the Lord and His Rest, so *COME*...My son and my daughter, *COME*,...Remember the emphasis is to COME, not to THINK. I am speaking to your spirit, not your mind. I realize that you may not have a frame of reference for walking out on the waters of faith, and Reaching out to me with your spirit. Remember, I AM bidding you to COME, all I ask is that you Reach with your spirit in faith and patience, and I will give you Rest. Be still, and know that I am God, and I will do the rest. *I call you into my Rest for the release of every burden of heart, mind and soul, Spirit to spirit I meet with you. R E A C H...*

E*xtend your heart to me*, *extend your faith towards me, extend your love towards me*, you are approaching and entering into my Rest (even before you arrive at my feet)...Come further into my room (the realm of Glory outshining from my person), my bosom, my heart is oh so open to you...**break the barriers of impatience, breach the barriers to intimacy, breach the barriers of unbelief,** and come further into my room (the realm of Glory outshining from my person). ***Be still***.

As you begin to receive my Rest, it will overwhelm you, endure my gift and let it consume your burdens, your fears and stresses...Nothing that opposes my Kingdom can remain when you encounter my Rest, you are coming into my Kingdom, you will experience my Order and my Peace, not as the world gives, MY Peace...Overwhelmed, Overwhelmed in the presence of my Grace. Overwhelmed in the presence of your King. Overwhelmed in the presence of My Rest...

Fear, it has no power here. Fear, it has no power to afflict when you are near to me. So I clothe you in the presence of my Rest. So I fill you with the Glory of my Rest. Remain extended, reaching for my Glory...Rest, Focus, COME...

Access your *inheritance*, where every yoke of fear is broken. Yes, Fear is unconstitutional within my Kingdom...Now be purged of the residue of fear in your members, be purged of the residue of fear in your subconscious, now be purged of the residue of fear in your dream life, thoughts and imaginations...Wash now in the presence of my Glory...Wash now in the Glory of my Rest, I am here...surrender to my Rest, it is conquering your enemies and vanquishing your fears...Only surrender to my Rest...surrender to my Rest, surrender to my Rest...believe, extend, access...Place no time frames on this encounter, be synchronized to the movements of my Kingdom. My Rest transcends time, it has no captivities or restraints, no burdens or limits, no obligations or deadlines, these are earthly distractions. My Rest is *Glory*, released from my being, from everlasting to everlasting, *I AM* Alpha and Omega, time has no dominion over my Rest... Only position yourself, and receive...

Come daily for more 'til all you know is my Rest...As my Rest arises, do not neglect to come my child (this is where some will miss it), continue to come, and you will remain filled with my Rest...This Kingdom Dominion of Rest is fastening itself to your life from this very moment...It will make itself known, for it is a part of me, my abiding presence upon you manifesting in Rest...REACH, as often as you come I will meet you with a measure of my tangible Rest...*COME TO THE TREE OF LIFE AND EAT OF ME*...**Now wait in my presence** until there is a tangible manifestation of my Glorious Rest...**Let nothing distract**, give no place to doubt...**REACH** and Receive... Wait, receive, receive...

Believe, Reach, Receive

A Biblical example of Reaching

And a certain woman, which had an issue of blood twelve years, And had suffered many things of many physicians, and had spent all that she had, and was nothing bettered, but rather grew worse, When she had heard of Jesus, came in the press behind, and touched his garment. For she said, If I may touch but his clothes, I shall be whole. And straightway the fountain of her blood was dried up; and she felt in her body that she was healed of that plague. **Mark 5:25-29**

The parallels are real. This is a great example for us to use for REACHING for His Rest. This woman had to press through the commotion of a frantic crowd; she had to press through the emotion of 12 years of pain; she had to press through the opinions of those who stigmatized her as unclean; she had to press through the doubt of twelve years of failure; she had to press through to revelation of the power of the Priesthood; she had to press through to understand the gravity of the anointing flowing downward from Aaron's beard to his skirts (the Hem of his garment) see *Psalms 133:2*. Surely she understood that Jesus was greater than Aaron, (SO SHE **REACHED** FOR THE HEM OF HIS GARMENT) and she received a miracle of healing.

Healing is the Children's Bread. Christ's anointing was unparalleled throughout all generations (being that living bread which came down from heaven). Bread for the hungry, the Bread of Life dipped in oil (ANOINTING, GLORY, HEALING AND REST). She was drawn in by the power and the aroma of his love. She was pulled in by the brightness of his Glory. Through a simple act of REACHING (in Faith), she received a glorious healing miracle. At the touch of his garment she was gloriously healed...

Never had there been an example of such a press, such a REACH, in scripture. She had no patterns to follow. She became the pattern, she established the precedent, that one could be healed by touching a garment...

Her press was beyond reason, beyond logic, beyond fear, beyond denominational bylaws, beyond doctrine, beyond hope, beyond popular opinion, beyond her symptoms which had grown worse...And she obtained favor, and she obtained healing, and she obtained grace and mercy and comfort at the touch of a garment worn by a King.

...and his rest shall be glorious. **Isaiah 11:10**

~List every detail of your encounter in your Rest Notes, even the most subtle changes. His Rest and Glory are tangible and real, many have experienced profound measures of His supernatural Rest like waves of an ocean. Your experience will be just as real; you are responding to His Invitation; and remember to take off the thinking cap...just come, and come again...He will meet you

Take the time to describe your experience with His Rest, these notes will encourage you as they increase in volume and reality, in Spirit and in Truth. His Rest is Glorious!

Take the time to describe your experience with His Rest, these notes will encourage you as they increase in volume and reality, in Spirit and in Truth. His Rest is Glorious!

But now the LORD my God hath given me **rest** *on every side, so that there is neither adversary*

nor evil occurrent (impact).

1 Kings 5:4

Jesus has been interceding for you, he is giving Rest to your land today!

MINDLESSNESS

Class #2 | To be spiritually minded is life

Obtaining His Rest is *AN EASY PROCESS*, when we get out of our heads. The invitation is to COME, not to think, calculate or reason. We don't have a frame of reference for His Rest until we've encountered it, so let's concentrate on simply COMING! **[Demonstrate the act of *COMING* with 2 participants, without telling them what they are coming for]** The word COME means to approach, move toward, draw closer, get nearer, to accompany...to show up! The Lord is saying "get over here" son or daughter, you're thinking way too much and that's a hindrance to receiving my Rest. It's time to drop everything, yes everything...even the hard stuff. doctors reports, financial concerns, life issues, family, ministry and work concerns, world events etc., ...Give me these next most precious moments of time to prepare you to COME.

I'm going to provide the Rest, so don't get worried if you don't feel anything yet, that's my part. Your first instruction is to stop thinking; I need your spirit not your mind. **[Demonstrate the act of *REACHING* with your spirit]** Your spirit is where I will attach my Glorious Rest. This will consume all that rages throughout your soul. All I need you to do is COME. Think of it this way, when I bid Peter to walk on turbulent waters, all he could do was COME...It was my Word that he walked out on. He was

{Bold areas with brackets can be used for group demonstrations} upheld by my Word as he walked on the waters, and did not start sinkin' until he started thinkin'!

And when the disciples saw him walking on the sea, they were troubled, saying, It is a spirit; <u>and they cried out for fear</u>. But straightway Jesus spake unto them, saying, Be of good cheer; it is I; <u>be not afraid</u>...

The first thing we notice here is that Jesus has mastered the turbulent waters. He walks effortlessly upon them, ruling the Waters by His Rest. Now, this should have been a tremendous encounter for the disciples, seeing Jesus walking on the waters, but they were unfamiliar with Jesus walking in this dimension of authority, somehow, it was easier for them to believe that he was a ghost! **[Demonstrate the act of *REACHING* with your spirit, with multiple distractions on both sides (need 2 volunteers)]**

There are many things within us that need to be adjusted because of our conformities to this world, superstitions, learned limitations and the prevalence of false teachings. Son or Daughter, can you see yourself walking upon the waters, even ruling them? Yes, I know that this question causes us to wrestle with what's possible. We'll have to lose *our* minds, and yield to His Word in order to do so! In like manner, God's Glory and Rest afford us many unusual and unprecedented opportunities to experience new dimensions of Kingdom Reality as they free us from learned limitations.

*And Peter answered him and said, Lord, if it be thou, **bid me come unto thee on the water**. And he said, **Come**. And when Peter was come down out of the ship, he walked on the water, to go to Jesus. But when he saw the wind boisterous, he was afraid; and beginning to sink, he cried, saying, Lord, save me. And immediately Jesus stretched forth his hand, and caught him, and said unto him, O thou of little faith, wherefore didst thou doubt?*

Matthew 14:26-31

Here we see a very famous invitation to COME, and while Peter did walk out on that Word, he was distracted by the winds. This reveals an important secret to obtaining the miraculous... <u>We need to limit our focus to COMING</u> (to Jesus), then, should a windfall of thoughts begin to swirl in our minds, we need not panic, but to maintain a singular focus, "Lord you told me to come". During my first encounter with His Rest, I was entirely focused on coming to Jesus for His Rest, even when I felt nothing change. [I did not succumb to reasoning, my spirit was locked in on Jesus] **[Demonstrate the act of *REACHING* with your spirit with a crowd of people blowing like the wind making noise]**

Somehow I knew within my spirit that there was more available than I had ever been taught or shown. Much like the woman with the issue of blood in Matthew Chapter 9, I said within myself (Lord, I am coming for your Rest), and reached beyond myself into a supernatural encounter with the Glory and Rest of God! My faith and desperation connected me to His Glory and Rest. This is where it all began...

Rabboni: The School of His Rest

Overview

Class #2 - New Discoveries: Extending your spirit and encountering the Lord Jesus Christ and His Rest

Training the human spirit to access Jesus Christ

- *Without Distraction*
- *With Distraction*
- *With Immense Distraction*

- *Without carnal thought or demonic imagination (Rest is a girdle for the loins of the mind) 1 Peter 1:13*
- *Without being distracted by visual or audible stimulation (Applying the "mute button", this is progressively attained)*

What is Spirit over mind renewal?

- *Where we are re-trained in the initial Order of things*
- *(spirit over mind)*
- *Taking our spiritual positions in Liberty through illumination*
- *Seeing the utter foolishness of following the carnal thought pattern*
- *Encountering the Lord at will*
- *Touching His Glory at will*
- *Carrying His Glory and Rest*
- *(Rest brings Order) Spirit over mind renewal*

Learning from Rabonni, who always cooperated with the Father

- *Whatever I see the Father do*

For a Christian, touching Jesus ought to be easier than touching any human being.

WEIGHTLESSNESS

Class #3 | Laying aside every weight

Wherefore seeing we also are compassed about with so great a cloud of witnesses, let us lay aside every weight, and the sin which doth so easily beset us, and let us run with patience the race that is set before us, **Hebrews 12:1**

Multitudes of believer's have tried to figure this one out for years. Is it really possible to lay aside "every weight"? It will be necessary, if we are going to run with patience the race that is set before us. Is there really a way to truly be free from spiritual, emotional, and even physical weights? Well, since we know that God cannot lie, the real question then becomes, "how do we do it"? Yes, *"we can do all things through Christ who strengthens us"*; but more specifically, Christ points us to a "Root Solution" for every directive. We covered "Root Solutions" in the Book "His Rest is Glorious".

The Christian life is an amazing journey of love and trial, intimacy and warfare. God's Word contains everything we need for victorious living. Many anointed verses of scripture are inadvertently "passed over" because we simply have not meditated upon their meaning. This is why I believe that every believer should read through and apply the teachings of Jesus Christ in the Gospels first, before delving into the Apostolic writings. Jesus gives "Root Solutions" to the many Apostolic admonitions and commands in scripture. Without these "Root Solutions", we would miss out on the powerful benefits of many verses.

In the opening verse of scripture we are admonished to *"lay aside every weight, and the sin that so easily besets us"*. This implies that weights (that are attached to our souls) can be connected to besetting sins (committed under oppression and heaviness). These weights are contributing to life's pressures, burdens and a sense of overall unrest. Because of this, it is vital that we grasp the truth and walk in the reality of weightlessness.

Gravity is defined as the force that attracts two bodies together. This force exists everywhere. Weightlessness happens when all **contact forces (supports, weights, burdens, etc.)** are removed. The Almighty God, who created the Law of Gravity to maintain Order and Rest in the universe, is the Lord over all forms of Gravity. **[Demonstrate contact forces and how they work]**

When God's Glory (which is defined as His ***weighty presence***) attaches itself to our beings, it separates all contact forces from our fragile souls. It counteracts the Laws of Gravity in our souls. You see, we have too many things weighing us down, burdening our lives, unsettling our souls. The Soul of man can experience a downward pull of gravity that can make us feel like we are carrying the world on our shoulders. David knew something about the downward pull of the soul.

Why art thou cast down, O my soul? and why art thou

disquieted within me? hope thou in God: for I shall yet praise him, who is the health of my countenance, and my God. **Psalms 42:11**

The answer to the question "why" varies with every person, but the experience of a weighed down soul is common to all. David spoke to his own soul and commanded it to *"hope thou in God"*. Hope is a huge Word! It is one of the abiding things, one of the eternal substances given to us by God. Without it, we would not be able to find our way out of dark places. The Rest of God is very often the first step on the way back to hopefulness. (See the Chapter "Weakness and Rest" in my book "His Rest is Glorious: Reaching the Anointing That Arrests All Fear".

And now abideth faith, hope, charity, these three; but the greatest of these is charity. **1 Corinthians 13:13**

The Rest of God is a preserver of Hope

Hopelessness is not in the vocabulary of the Kingdom of God. The feeling of hopelessness, however, is a common occurrence with mankind. For me, it is one of the gravest sensations, the darkest experiences of the human soul. It is a dark cloud that veils the Sun, and dampens the light. No one can live under a continuous shadow of hopelessness.

David knew that God would pierce his darkest hours with the amazing light of His Glory; thereby diffusing hopelessness and restoring faith and hope again. His weighty presence is an invasion of light, lifting us out of the dark night of our soul.

Declaration: Veil of hopelessness be removed in Jesus name! Light of Hope shine forth the Brightness of my Father's Glory!

Just a quick note: Praise and Worship tends to reverse the gravitational pull, and our God is the Glory and the lifter of our heads! As His Rest begins to manifest within your soul, and you begin to praise Him, there comes a lifting of our heads from He who is the health of our countenance, and our God! We then begin to understand (experientially) the meaning of these words...

> *Lord, how are they increased that trouble me! many are they that rise up against me. Many there be which say of my soul, There is no help for him in God. Selah. <u>But thou, O LORD, art a shield for me; my glory, and the lifter up of mine head.</u>*
>
> **Psalm 3:1-3**

We've sung the song, and heard the teaching, but now in this time we are entering into an age of actuality! *"But thou, O Lord, art a shield for me"*. A shield that protects, a shield that covers, a shield that repels the darts! In the Testimony of my first encounter with His Glorious Rest, I experienced this shield. It is a literal shield, forged from God's own Glory, an impenetrable substance of His being. I experienced this shield immediately after my encounter with Jesus, and none of the arrows, anchors or darts of the wicked one could pierce it. We have heard much teaching about the Shield of Faith, but when His Rest encounters us, we are surrounded by a tangible Shield of Glory.

God's Glory creates a sense of weightlessness, bringing heavens atmosphere of freedom into our lives (our immediate atmosphere). We see this demonstrated physically often times in scripture when the Lord wills. Jesus (*ascended into Heaven Acts 1:9-11*), Enoch (*was translated into Heaven Hebrews 11:5*), Elijah (*was caught up into Heaven 2 Kings 2:11*), Phillip (*was caught away Acts 8:39-40*), Peter (*walked on water Matthew 14:29*) and John the Apostle (*was caught up to Heaven Revelation 4:1-3*) just to name a few. In these instances, the laws of gravity where counteracted and overthrown. Could God's use of bodily translation utilize the same principles of weightlessness? That one is still a mystery.

Natural Example: We only feel our weight when we are standing on the ground, or sitting in a chair, but never when we are suspended in the air after jumping on a trampoline. The reason for this is because when we are suspended in mid air, we have ***no contact*** with anything. I had the unwanted experience of weightlessness while falling four stories in 1986. My sense of weightlessness was immediately halted when I landed on a concrete slab. When the force of my falling body met with the ***contact force*** of the concrete beneath me, my sense of weightlessness was removed.

The Rest and Glory of God removes the unwanted contact forces of life that press in upon our souls continually. Pain, fear, worries, traumas, struggles, burdens, trials, problems, warfare, pressures, issues, and concerns of every kind etc., all make contact with the soul [they manifest as weights]. The Rest of God acts as a barrier (a Shield) between us and the many sources of unrest, resulting in a sense of weightlessness. What is so powerful about this is the fact that God's Rest (Glory) is actually His *weighty presence*.

The weight of God's presence makes us lighter. This is almost always the result when praying for people under the anointing of the Holy Spirit, or under the Presence of God's Glory. People commonly say... "I feel lighter"! The reason for this is that God's Glory or the anointing of the Holy Spirit, whichever is manifesting, removes the unwanted spiritual, emotional, or physical contacts creating heaviness and unrest.

Yes, the weighty presence of God counteracts the power of troubles to pull us downward, and holds us up, keeping all contact forces at bay, enabling weightlessness (a sense of total emotional freedom, and spiritual breakthrough).

Have you ever seen video footage of astronauts experiencing weightlessness in a spacecraft? This happens when all of the right conditions are met. The Rest of God is the foundation of weightless living, it is the delivery system for a life free from burdens and pressures, even when there are troubles on every side. The underlined portions of the scripture below could only be the direct result of God's Rest!

> *But we have this treasure in earthen vessels, that the excellency of the power may be of God, and not of us. We are troubled on every side, **yet not distressed**; we are perplexed, **but not in despair;** Persecuted, **but not forsaken**; cast down, **but not destroyed;** Always bearing about in the body the dying of the Lord Jesus, **that the life also of Jesus might be made manifest in our body**.* **2 Corinthians 4:7-10**

What is the life of Jesus spoken of here? Well, it is clearly not his physical life. That life had an end, and was forever changed when resurrected. No, the life referred to here is that essential life. The Substance of His Being. The Word of Life, immeasurable, ingenerate and incorruptible. A fusion of Glory and Love. Remember, His Rest is Glory. When we receive His Rest, we'll obtain a testimony over stress:

- Not destroyed
- Not forsaken
- Not distressed
- Not in despair

> *In him was life; and the life was the light of men* **John 1:4**

His Rest is a well of Life, tapping into the ocean from which many waters of truth flow. This is Jesus Christ Himself. He is the Truth! Christ Himself is the very Rest that he offers. He is a Life-Giving Spirit.

And so it is written, The first man Adam was made a living soul; the last Adam was made a quickening spirit.
1 Corinthians 15:45

He is the Lord of the Sabbath [Matt 12:8]. He is the Word of God, the Light of the World and His Rest is Glorious!

For God, who commanded the light (actual light like the rays of the sun) to shine out of darkness, hath shined in our hearts, to give the light (illumination) of the knowledge of the glory (Doxa) of God in the face of Jesus Christ. **2 Corinthians 4:6**

For me, the knowledge of the Glory of His Rest came this very same way, through an actual encounter with him. He shined into my heart and brought illumination of His Rest to my whole creation. This is what I needed, and what you need, illumination [meaning to clarify, reveal and give understanding to]. As you R.E.A.C.H. for His Rest you are going to experience a measure of God's Glory and Splendor in the face of Jesus Christ. Don't settle for less, continue to R.E.A.C.H. for His Rest until you experience the manifestation of weightlessness. It's *REAL*!

Prayer over you: Father God, you did not create man for burden and weights, bondage and slavery; nonetheless, we have been enslaved in so many ways. Help us to hear the call of the Lord Jesus Christ to Come unto him, and to receive His Rest. I pray for illumination that leads to a transforming encounter with your Rest for every man and woman reading this book; and for everyone that they encounter with your Rest. Father God, I ask that you would allow each one to experience weightlessness to such a degree, that it would be as if each one were walking 6 inches off of the ground ...weightless and worry free!

Select two participants from among those that have obtained His Rest, and have them to impart a measure of His Rest and Glory to others.
(as a boost*)*

This is the Rest Collective

A People living in and Imparting Rest
To the Body and to the Nations

Overview

Class #3 was intentionally and primarily about encounter, this is the most effective way to arrive at weightlessness

Primary means of encounter

- *The Holy Spirit manifesting Glory through any Sovereign means*
- *Personal or Secondary anointed prayer from a brother or sister in Christ manifesting in Rest and Glory*
- *Secondary or Personal prayer is unnecessary with <u>personal visitation from the Lord Jesus Christ</u>*

Rest Teams ministering to the Rest Collective

REQUIREMENTS

Touch
- *The manifestation of His Glory and Rest*

Detachment
- *The separation of various contact forces, spiritual, emotional, even physical from our beings*

(Demonstrate touch and detachment, and the manifestation of weightlessness with 2 participants)

For the LORD shall comfort Zion: he will comfort all her waste places; and he will make her wilderness like Eden, and her desert like the garden of the LORD; <u>joy and gladness shall be found therein</u>, thanksgiving, and the voice of melody. Hearken unto me, my people; and give ear unto me, O my nation: for a law shall proceed from me, and I will make my judgment **to rest for a light of the people.**

Isaiah 51:3-4

Jesus has been interceding for you, he is giving Rest to your land today!

TIMELESSNESS

Class #4 | Time: Slave or Master

Time is a unit of measure between events past, present and future, and when we fail to measure it exactly [which we all do]; it can become a source of internal and external unrest. The thing about time is that, while it is exact, and waits for no one, the circumstances of life are ever-changing, and rarely predictable. Yes time keeps on moving, even when we are delayed.

How many times have you been held up by traffic, automobile breakdowns or unforeseen emergencies? It is often in these kinds of situations that we refer to ourselves as being "*pressed* for time", "*running* late", "*falling* behind", "*strapped for time*" or "*swamped*". Some would say that the answer is practicing better time management, but that still doesn't provide help for the unforeseen events of life. The only one who can subvert the mastery of time is the Everlasting and Eternal God Himself. Time is a servant of God, and not the other way around!

Have you ever heard the saying "marching to the beat of a different drummer"? Having played drums in a marching band while I was in Junior High School, I learned that timing was our responsibility. The Drummers were the ones who determined and maintained the tempo of the songs, which kept the band playing and marching in unison. If we drummers would have strayed off beat, the whole band would have fallen into a chaotic frenzy. In order to march to the beat of a different drummer, we must first break free from the cadence and tempo of the band, the crowd, the masses [the rudiments of this world]. [Demonstrate Kingdom Arrhythmia | Marching to the rhythms of the Kingdom]

Beware lest any man spoil you through philosophy and vain deceit, after the tradition of men, after the rudiments of the world, and not after Christ. **Colossians 2:8**

Philosophies, vain deceits, and traditions of men can cause us to miss out on the *Kairos* of God. A *Kairos* moment is a moment of appointment, action and spontaneity. This would be altogether in contrast to a rudimentary moment, which is pre-planned and full of repetition. In drumming, a rudiment is a basic drum pattern. These rudiments would be practiced over and over until they were *perfected, until they became second nature...* Off to work, pick up the kids, home for dinner, time for the favorite TV show, then off to bed...Back to work etc., etc. Now don't get me wrong, there are certainly many earthly appointments and duties that we need to be prompt about, and there is also the idea of decency and order. We are not putting time on trial, it is slavery to time that we are addressing. The *Spirit of Preoccupation* is robbing us of peace and fellowship with the I AM [who is eternally present]. He is **always on time**, even when it appears that He's late!

Have you ever prayed for an hour, hoping to hear His voice, and heard nothing; only to get into your car and have an encounter with Him while you are driving! God is not on our clock, He is Eternal, and Everlasting, without beginning or Ending, Alpha and Omega all at the same time! Glory! He never needs to hurry, He's already there!

In the Rest of God there is an enormous awareness of God's presence, direction, manifestation and attendance to us, as *Immanuel* (God with us). In order for us to remain God conscious [in the present tense], we need to be preoccupied with God, moving in the freedom of His tangible presence, even when we are considerate of time. My new motto is that while I am "considerate to time", I don't worship it, I Worship God! I cannot serve two Masters!

As someone who once was habitually late for appointments, I would constantly hear it from my wife about my word and integrity being compromised when I arrived late. I found it very hard to serve under the confines of earthly timeframes, maybe this is why I chose self-employment most of my life prior to ministry. I just couldn't get it together, the harder I tried, the later I would arrive. Anxiety surely had a part to play in this. Amazingly, when I decided to break free from the confines of time, and it's pressures, stresses and bondages, and began to live and move in the Rest of God, I began to be on time, unstressed, and better prepared for my scheduled tasks.

I found that in the REST OF GOD, I was simply more effective and productive at everything [His Rest is Glorious]. A few practical changes made all the difference for me. For one, I simply stopped committing to a specific time for most appointments, but rather, committed to a range of time, leaving room for any unforeseen circumstances, and even a few spontaneous encounters with the Lord. I then began to consciously walk in His Rest while preparing for each task, this allowed the weights [anxieties, pressures and stresses] to fall off, and relieved the sensation of time pulling against my soul [creating weight]. It was the freedom of timelessness which produced the blessing of timeliness! Remember, God is never in a hurry, He's already there at every future point in time.

The Bible uses the word "time" 620 times, but many of these uses are given from the perspective of God's intended timing, relating to God's purposes. Whether it be an "appointed time", "set time", "prophetic time", "purposed time", "process of time", "the time of life", "times and seasons", "the fullness of time" or "event based time"...God is always in authority and dominion over time! I would say that it's "High Time" for us to begin to live out our days on "Kingdom Time"; giving more time to obtaining His Rest/ Glory. This must become our New Life Priority, Marching to the beat of the Rhythms of the Kingdom.

Are you Living on Borrowed Time or Kingdom Time?

Let's Explore the Difference…

"Borrowed time" implies that you could have died some time ago, but are not aware of the reasons why you didn't, counting the days until the inevitable happens...

"Kingdom Time", on the other hand denotes that; though you could have died some time ago, you have factored in (Because God has chosen, and loved you) the intervention of God through our Lord Jesus Christ and His Mighty Army of Angels...You would not have seen twenty, thirty, forty, fifty, sixty etc., if it were not for the intervention of God...When you are Living on Kingdom Time, the One who controls TIME, invades TIME, and changes the outcome of potentially hazardous situations...Whether you are looking back or looking forward KINGDOM TIME factors into your present existence in the earth. You may have been told that you don't have long to live, or that you have a condition that threatens your lifespan...The Devil is a Liar...

Make this declaration with me

- **I am living on Kingdom Time, not borrowed time**
- **I am under the Dominion of my Father's Eternal Life; the Very Life of The Lord Jesus Christ is resident within me.**

Always bearing about in the body the dying of the Lord Jesus, that **the life** *also of Jesus* **might be made manifest in our body.** **2 Corinthians 4:10**

And it shall come to pass in the day that the LORD shall give thee **rest** from thy sorrow, **<u>and from thy fear...</u>**

Isaiah 14:3

Jesus has been interceding for you, he is giving Rest to your land today!

PROCRASTINATION

Class #5 | Enemies of the Pioneering Spirit

If Rest is at the center of the spectrum, then procrastination and perfectionism are at both ends of the spectrum of time. Both of these phenomenon are Rest *antagonists*. They are both in opposition to Rest, and are indicators of unrest. Procrastination (taking too long to do a thing, or putting off 'til tomorrow, what could be accomplished today) can sometimes be rooted in the undercurrent of unrest (that we call) anxiety. Things just keep getting pushed back further and further, piling up to the ceiling 'til the inevitable happens: It all comes tumbling down. Very often, unrest robs us of the necessary peace needed to complete simple tasks.

Three weeks of laundry, six nights of take-out orders, gas tank's on empty, and the grass is taller than the hedges. What looks like gross disorder is often a manifestation of procrastination rooted in unrest.

The more we move in the Rest of God, the more we see that it is rooted in virtually every area of life and ministry. This is why, once again, we call His Rest both foundational (a necessary and essential part of our functional existence), and positional (the place from which every Kingdom attribute, anointing, gifting and calling receives it's greatest stability and support). Very often all we need to do to help a person who is experiencing great disorder in their lives, is to release into them the dominion of His Rest. When we tackle these problems at the root, procrastination moves over to the center toward Rest.

Your most productive days are your days of Rest! Yes, I know that sounds contrary to reason, but productivity is not a product of labor, it is a product of efficiency, which is a maximized in Rest. Oh, Hallelujah! Teach us Lord, Remember, this is Rabboni's School, he makes all the rules!

I used to be a prolific procrastinator, but since I got a hold of His Rest, or I should say, His Rest got a hold of me, I am more productive than ever. His Rest has made room for the Pioneering Spirit within me to flourish and become fruitful... All for His Glory, all for His Name!

Prayer: I release the dominion of His Rest into your mind, taking permanent dominion over procrastination and disorder in Jesus name. Receive the Rest of the Lord Jesus Christ.

Response: Thank you Lord, I receive your Rest..Wait on Him...receive...I am free from procrastination, and will remain free as I pursue you in your Rest. Lord, penetrate to my deepest parts with your tangible Rest. Touch with your Glory, heal every underlying wound causing fear, and subdue all that is born from unrest.

I receive the Rest of the Lord Jesus Christ.
Wait, receive, be filled, here comes the bubble, Glory

PERFECTIONISM
Class #6 | Enemies of the Pioneering Spirit

Whereas procrastination is taking too long to begin something, perfectionism can result in taking too long to complete something, once you've begun. Both of these are enemies of the pioneering spirit, and manifestations of unrest.

Perfectionism stems from a kind of overanalyzing, second guessing, critical mindset. This is very closely associated with fear, which often births a sense of having to be perfect, which would create unrest in anyone! This is sometimes described as performance anxiety; I believe that I suffered from this form of unrest for many years.

As a Record Producer, I once spent nearly 3 years working on a project, only to find out that the earliest renditions of the song were the most *anointed*. The more [I] tried to perfect the song musically and audibly, [depending upon my finite senses, which were steeped in unrest] the more I doubted my own ability to produce it. The changes were constant, the uncertainty was continuous, and when I'd finally come to a place of satisfaction, something in me would scream "I can make it better"!!! And back to the drawing board I went.

I hadn't encountered His Rest back then, even though I had loved the Lord for many years and had seen countless miracles. To think, a seemingly simple thing like Rest, became the catalyst for freedom in untold areas of my life. His Rest changed my perspective of perfection. It doesn't look like it used to. It's been redefined through rested eyes, and a rested heart. Oh, that the Lord would give us eyes to see beyond the visible, and Rest to enter into, to perceive, and to experience the very mysteries of the Kingdom of Heaven. We are missing out on so much. Jesus Come, Rest Come, we need you.

For he shall grow up before him as a tender plant, and as a root out of a dry ground: he hath no form nor comeliness; and when we shall see him, there is no beauty that we should desire him. **Isaiah 53:2**

How many beautiful people [those with visible flaws, we all have them] have we rejected because of a spirit of perfectionism operating within us? How many ministries have we discounted because of the condition of the building, or the number of it's membership, or the way the Pastor looks. Outward judgments and criticisms born from our own internal unrest. Often times people who are always trying to fix something about you, are actually suffering from a strong sense of inadequacy, born from rejection which produces unrest. When these people receive and encounter His Rest, they often become complete in themselves, at Rest with who they are in Christ, and then they are able to perceive the beauty of others, just the way they are.

Undoubtedly, the Prophet Isaiah was prophesying to the

religious leaders of Christ's day when he said *"there is no beauty that we should desire him"*. By their stern adherence to the law, and their pious perspectives, they would easily qualify as perfectionists. And because of this, they did not perceive the beauty of the Perfect One.

Perfectionism places way too much emphasis on our own ability to communicate or complete a task, and not enough emphasis on God's ability to persuade, compel, intervene, arouse, encounter, illuminate, adjust, interpret, and to intercede for us, opening the necessary doors of favor. Every one of God's Pioneers needed this kind of assistance from the Lord. He is the Pioneer of Pioneers. Heaven is His Throne, and the earth is His footstool. Our Best will be assured, when our Rest is prioritized. R.E.A.C.H. for the Glory That Arrests All Fear.

Overview

Class # 4,5,6 Challenging our priorities, breaking free from the Dominion of Time, while remaining conscious of it

This is mandatory if we are going to live under the Dominion of His Rest

Break free from the timetables of others whenever possible Move to the rhythm of the Kingdom

Sample: *"We're having dinner at 7:00pm, do you think you can make it"? Truth: You can make it if you shift priorities and use that block of time for dinner, and leave your son's basketball game at half-time. Now you have pressure and disappointment. Disappointment because you couldn't fulfill the expectations or obligations of both parties, and their particular demand upon your time...This is a setup for unrest. Priorities are very closely related to Order. People pleasers will always have a problem maintaining Order in their lives.*

Most of us would look at the above mentioned example as an easy decision, because our children rank high on our list of priorities. Right? A simple resolution might be to take a rain check for dinner, and live in the Rest of a happy child, and the bliss of that decision. His yoke is easy! His burden is light!

Living in the Rest of God, *means that as much as possible we avoid placing ourselves in pressure filled situations, unless they are critical to life or emergencies. Living on Kingdom time means* *that if at all possible we avoid social traps. As Christians we are to be led by the Holy Spirit, order our priorities, and not be constrained through obligation. This does not mean that we are stuck on being comfortable , or that we should not be willing to make sacrifices. Nor does it mean that we are not to engage socially, we are the light of the world... It simply means that we are to be regulated by Rest and Glory, and not by constraint, pressure and worry. Time must become a slave to the Rest of God.*

...Remember timeframes are another source of attachment and can produce great weights and bonds.

In Rest, Patience thrives, and Order is Sustained

Let no man beguile you:

- *Pull you out of your appointment with Rest, sometimes this means not answering the phone (Turn off the cell phone, it can become a Rest stealer)*

- *Be synchronized with Heaven, Jesus was*

Then answered Jesus and said unto them, Verily, verily, I say unto you, The Son can do nothing of himself, but what he seeth the Father do: for what things soever he doeth, these also doeth the Son likewise. **John 5:19**

- *Half-Speed: See the Testimony of my first encounter with His Glorious Rest in* **His Rest is Glorious: Reaching the Glory that Arrests All Fear...** It outlines how His Rest can manifest so tangibly that the world around us appears to be moving at half-speed.

- *Walking in His Rest cures Procrastination and Perfectionism*

The LORD said unto my Lord, <u>Sit thou</u> (*a picture of Rest and Order*) at my right hand, until I make thine enemies **<u>thy footstool</u>**.

Psalms 110:1

FEARLESSNESS

Class #7 | Getting our heads into the clouds

Almost 20 Years ago, my wife was visited in the night by an angel dressed in white. He raised one leg and slammed it to the ground, twisting his foot side to side as if he was putting out a cigarette...and this is what he said "Do not fear the enemy".

Most fear is delivered to the mind first, to the rational realm of thought and reason. In the world, there is a common saying…"Get your head out of the clouds", in other words, "get back to the rational", "stop dreaming". "Pay attention"! Well I want to make a radical statement to begin this section of teaching….We need to get our heads back into the clouds, The Cloud of Glory! The realm of reason gives easy opportunity for knowledge traps to be set.

But thou, O Lord, art a shield for me; my glory, and the lifter up of mine head. **Psalms 3:3**

The realm of Glory transcends knowledge

...to know the Love of Christ which passeth knowledge, that ye might be filled with all the fullness of God.

Ephesians 3:19

This passage of scripture seems to indicate that the fullness of God is somewhere beyond the realm of knowledge. And when we are filled with all the fullness of God, we will arise to God's own posture towards fear. The result for us would simply be "FEARLESSNESS". Yes, the Father wants His children to have a *fearless* existence!

We must understand that virtually everything in the visible realm is subject to knowledge (learned facts, information and reason), and therefore subject to fear, which came by the tree of knowledge. It ensnared man because of his need to know so much, especially after discovering so much. The more we learned, the more we sought reassurance through knowledge. The more we learned, the more we leaned on knowledge. Well, this presented the enemy with a gateway to unrest and fear, "simply tell them something, and they will run down the path of knowledge. And while on that path, I will steer them away from their greatest asset…The Glory and Rest of God".

If the truth be told, we are often mistakenly dependent upon our *knowledge* of God, without having encountered the realities it provides. For instance,

Isaiah 41:10 says:

Fear thou not; for <u>I am with thee</u>: be not dismayed; for <u>I am thy God</u>: <u>I will strengthen thee</u>; yea, <u>I will help thee</u>; yea, <u>I will uphold thee with the right hand of my righteousness</u>.

The emphasis here is not our fear, it's God's Presence,

Person, Providence, Strength, Graciousness, Power and Righteousness. Let's take a closer look at these Divine qualities possessed by our Father. We must be moved beyond the realm of knowledge, into the realm of manifestation and encounter.

Grace and peace be multiplied unto you through <u>the knowledge of God, and of Jesus our Lord,</u> *According as his divine power hath given unto us all things that pertain unto life and godliness,* <u>through the knowledge of him</u> *that hath called us to* **glory and virtue**: **2 Peter 1:1-3**

Twice here in the above scripture we see knowledge as a bridge to manifestation, a conduit of reconstruction, and a vehicle for bringing truth into operation. The first manifestations would be multiplied grace and peace, after this, all things that pertain unto life and godliness, and ultimately the recovery of glory and virtue. This is the full working of the knowledge of God, and of Jesus our Lord... Moving His offspring toward total restoration, even the recovery of His Glory and Rest.

Glory reveals what knowledge declares

God declares, "Fear not, for I am with thee", this is what we call a promise. God is with us, so we don't have to fear. Wait a minute, I know that you are with me Father, Lord allow the knowledge of your presence to lead me into the Glory of your presence.

God's Glory manifests the I AM on the scene. While it is wonderful to be in the *Know*, I conclude that it is better to be in the *Now* (Rest, Glory and Manifest Presence). Fear has never had an argument with God Himself, but it has often challenged what I know.

CROSSING OVER THE SEA with JESUS

**FEAR NOT, HE IS NEAR, IAM WITH YOU,
I HAVE PLACED MY GLORY UPON YOU**

This is the prophetic Song resounding in my Spirit, so sweet the sound, so sweet the sound...manifested GLORY

**FEEL MY WAVES, FEEL MY LOVE
< FEEL MY PRESENCE HOLDING YOU UP
FEEL MY WAVES, FEEL MY LOVE
< FEEL MY PRESENCE HOLDING YOU UP
FEAR NOT | FEAR NOT | FEAR NOT | FEAR NOT
I REBUKE THE WINDS FOR YOU
AND STILL THE SEA
RECEIVE MY REST
LAY HOLD OF ME**

AS MY REST MANIFESTS, ASK FOR WHAT YOU WILL

Overview

Class #7 Fears most powerful element is the realm of knowledge and conclusions

It's second most powerful element is in the realm of sight and feeling

Living in the Clouds trumps the realm of knowledge based fear
Fear often argues with knowledge, but never with God
If we hang out with God more, we'll have less fear

What ever wins the fight for your senses,
wins the battle for your Rest

Though I have battled fear may times and come out on the losing side, It has not happened since my encounter with His Rest
I am undefeated since that day
And you will be too

The Lord will come and be glorified in His Saints
This is a Now Word as well as a future Word

- *Get your head up into the clouds so that you can see where your help comes from*
- *Get your head up into the clouds, so that you can be blinded by the light of the Son*
- *Get your head up into the clouds, so that you can see the panoramic view of the Kingdom of God*

There is nothing that can compete with that reality. When Stephen was stoned he saw the HEAVENS opened, and Jesus (Rabboni) standing at the right hand of the Father...I don't believe he had an ounce of Fear; I don't believe he even felt the pain of the Stones...He was surely Surrounded by Glory, and Saturated with His Rest as he prayed for his murderers.

His Rest is Glorious

Healing Rest

There is another wonderful benefit of His Rest and Glory, they manifest the perfect environment for divine healing. Sicknesses, Diseases, infirmities are all manifestations of unrest in the body…Even science credits stress for many diseases. His Rest is Glorious, it ravages unrest, yes every kind…He and His Rest are one…What did he do when he encountered disease? What happened when disease encountered Jesus? Which Disease did Jesus fail to heal?

Yes this is an all encompassing invitation, from Adam to Modern Saints, for every failure, every fallout from the Garden of Eden, every Curse. It's an all encompassing invitation. For your problem, for mine. Everything that Jesus did he did by love, from a position of Rest. His Rest is Glory.

ACTS 10:38

How God anointed Jesus of Nazareth with the Holy Ghost and with power, who went about doing good and healing all that were oppressed of the devil, for God was with Him. This oppression included every form of unrest known and unknown to man.

Reach, Touch, Heal…

For, when we were come into Macedonia, our flesh had **no rest**, but we were troubled on every side; without were fighting's, **within were fears**

2 Corinthians 7:5

This is the Hour to
LIVE IN HIS GLORY (REST)

We Want To Pray For You...

Occasionally there's a need for a "boost" in order to receive His Glorious Rest. We have rarely if ever prayed for anyone that did not receive a tangible manifestation of His Glorious Rest. Because of this, our hearts go out to every reader desiring to have the same encounter that we had. I have released a measure of His Rest by impartation to many that are now releasing the same impartation to others...We call this "a boost". It is allowable by the Lord, but He warned me to always send people directly to Him, He is the source, and His Rest is Glorious.

As the circle widens, those that are walking or desiring to walk in His Rest are enabled to impart a measure to others, just like us... We refer to this circle as **The Rest Collective.** JESUS is our source and yours, so we all must continue to encounter Him in HIS REST to remain free from the dominion of fear.

If you need a boost, and we are unable to get to you, we can send an anointed prayer cloth that has been prayed over as a point of contact. [Our contact info is on page 102 of this book] We are confident that you will be greatly benefited by it, and they are completely free. This is not a commercial effort, this is a desire to prepare a people for the days ahead, to adorn His Bride with a Garment of Rest and Glory.
Sincerely, Apostle Richard Taylor

attend to my words; *Proverbs 4:19-21*-**Rest notes**

Rabboni: The School of His Rest

attend to my words; <u>Proverbs 4:19-21</u>**-Rest notes**

attend to my words;** Proverbs 4:19-21**-Rest notes

attend to my words; <u>*Proverbs 4:19-21*</u>**-Rest notes**

Acknowledgements

Special thanks to my wife Estelle, my chief intercessor, woman of faith and best friend; to my Spiritual Mentor's over the past 25 years: Wade Taylor, Jay Francis, Matthew Caruso, Herbert Rylander and other great men and women of God who played a significant role in my life; to Denise Courts, Tony Flood and Brett Tompkins for spiritual seasonings; to Basil and Roxann Robinson for Apostolic impartations; to the Master's Table family for your love and support; to Richard K. Taylor Sr., Barney Christie, Anthony Christie, and to my mother Joyce Christie-Taylor for a mother's unending love, and the gift of writing; to my children (natural and spiritual sons and daughters) and grandchildren, I release a generational blessing of spiritual life... Above all I thank my Heavenly Father for the gift of His Son Jesus Christ, my Lord and Savior, and the presence of The Holy Spirit within my life and ministry.

Prayer of Salvation

Lord Jesus I ask you to come into my heart and fill my life with hope. I surrender to you Lord Jesus, and ask you to save me from my sins and fears. I believe that you died on the cross and rose again on the third day. I want to live for you because you died for me, thank you Lord for saving me. Thank you for your saving grace.

Other Published Books By Richard K. Taylor

- ### A Beauty Mark: The Mark of an Overcomer

"A Beauty Mark" is a Powerful Christian Devotional which explores and imparts the Divine perspective of beauty in weakness. As it delicately unveils our flaws (beauty marks), it asserts that God's Glory shines far brighter than does the visible flaw. It is from this perspective that the reader is encouraged to view/see ones own self and others. The Author contends that to attain perfection or flawlessness through any other means is akin to following Satan's deceptive road to independence. (History itself has taught us about the futility of mankind without God). As a reflector of God's own Light, he began to glory in his own beauty, not understanding the privilege of reflecting the beauty of God. "The Light was not his own, nor the reflection, only the privilege belonged to him". Engaging and riveting examples are taken from scripture and modern life depicting the beauty of God's embrace upon the broken and flawed. This book offers to it's readers a new pair of eyes, to embrace with God's love what was once despised. You will want to enjoy it again and again.

On Amazon.com & Barnesandnoble.com In paperback and kindle editions…

Other Published Books By Richard Taylor

- **GALL: Overcoming the Power of Dominating Emotions**

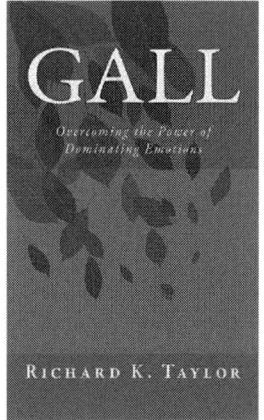

"Gall" is a victory lap for multitudes of people who are struggling with spiritual and emotional strongholds. This book exposes the spiritual root of such strongholds as Bitterness, Rejection, Shame, Self-Pity, Fear and Pride, while prescribing the appropriate antidotes. This groundbreaking revelatory masterpiece unfolds corners of untold truths for the equipping of this present generation, while presenting dynamic tools for sustained freedom from dominating emotions.

On Amazon.com & Barnesandnoble.com In paperback

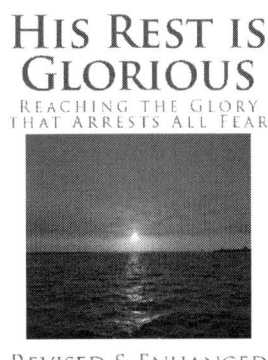

Other Published Books By Richard K. Taylor

His Rest is Glorious: Reaching the Glory That Arrests All Fear

His Rest is Glorious: Reaching The Glory That Arrests All Fear, is a roadmap into an actual encounter with the Rest of the Lord Jesus Christ. This is prompted by the invitation to "Come unto me, all ye that labour and are heavy laiden, and I will give you REST" Matthew 11:28-29 This Rest is tangible and actual, not conceptual or figurative. Amazing insights, revelations, and anointings are imparted page after page, as the reader is drawn into this dynamic teaching, and coached into the spiritual exercise of REACHING for the Anointing That Arrests All Fear. As this Anointing of Rest is received, it begins to establish the Kingdom Dominion of Rest as a literal hedge around our lives... If you've been embattled by fear, this is your time, your opportunity to receive freedom from it's harassing snare, once and for all... R E A C H

On Amazon.com & Barnesandnoble.com In paperback

CONTACT INFORMATION

Available For:
Ministry Bookings/Itinerary
Speaking Engagements/
Author Events/
Book Signings/
Call 860-206-0424
Author Website:
www.richardktaylor-author.com

Ministry Affiliation:
The Master's Table Ministries
Apostolic Leadership
Richard Taylor
(Apostolic Leader/Senior Pastor)
(860)768-2086
Estelle Taylor
(Prophetic/Pastoral)

P.O. Box 290290
Wethersfield, CT
(860) 206-0424
www.themasterslove.org

This is the Hour to
LIVE IN HIS GLORY (REST)

Made in the USA
Middletown, DE
12 April 2019